YOUR KNOWLEDGE HAS V.

- We will publish your bachelor's and master's thesis, essays and papers

- Your own eBook and book - sold worldwide in all relevant shops

- Earn money with each sale

Upload your text at www.GRIN.com
and publish for free

Imprint:

Copyright © 2008 GRIN Verlag, Open Publishing GmbH
Print and binding: Books on Demand GmbH, Norderstedt Germany
ISBN: 9783640575763

This book at GRIN:

http://www.grin.com/en/e-book/146637/the-day-of-the-week-and-the-month-of-the-year-effects-applications-of

Eleftherios Giovanis

The Day of the Week and the Month of the Year Effects: Applications of Rolling Regressions in EVIEWS and MATLAB

GRIN Publishing

GRIN - Your knowledge has value

Since its foundation in 1998, GRIN has specialized in publishing academic texts by students, college teachers and other academics as e-book and printed book. The website www.grin.com is an ideal platform for presenting term papers, final papers, scientific essays, dissertations and specialist books.

Visit us on the internet:

http://www.grin.com/

http://www.facebook.com/grincom

http://www.twitter.com/grin_com

The Day of the Week and the Month of the Year Effects: Applications of Rolling Regressions in EVIEWS and MATLAB

Eleftherios Giovanis

Abstract

In this paper we examine the calendar anomalies in the stock market index of Athens. Specifically we examine the day of the week and the month of the year effects, where we expect negative or lower returns on Monday and the highest average returns on Friday for the day of the week effect and the higher average returns in January, concerning the January effect. For the period we examine we found insignificant returns on Monday, but significant positive and higher average returns on Friday. Also our results are consistent with the literature for the month of the year effect, where we find the highest average returns in January. Furthermore we estimate with ordinary least squares (OLS) and symmetric and asymmetric Generalized Autoregressive Conditional Heteroskedasticity (GARCH) rolling regressions and we conclude that the week day returns are not constant through the time period we examine but are changed. Specifically, while in the first half-period of the rolling regression there are negative returns on Mondays so we observe the day of the week effecting, in the last half-period of the rolling regression Friday presents the highest returns, but the lowest returns are reported on Tuesday and not on Monday, indicating a change shift in the pattern of the day of the week effect. Full programming routines of rolling regressions in EVIEWS and MATLAB software are described.

1. Introduction

Many studies and researches have been made in calendar effects. One of them is the study of Aggarwal and Tandon (1994) test the day-of-the week found that Monday returns are negative in thirteen countries, but are significant only in seven countries. Also they found that Friday returns are significantly positive in almost all countries. Agathee (2008) examined the day of the week effect, who finds positive and significant ordinary least squares regression coefficients on Mondays, Wednesdays, Thursdays and Fridays, but however Fridays returns are the highest. Mills *et al.* (2000) haven't found Monday effect , but a Tuesday effect similar to other papers is presented. Aggarwal and Rivoli (1989) find that Monday and Tuesday returns are lower than the overall average, while the Friday returns are higher, as also the volatility measured by the standard deviation is highest on Mondays. So in addition to the Monday effect, Aggarwal and Rivoli (1989) find a Tuesday effect in four Asian markets, which examined. Draper and Paudyal (2002) FT-All Share index and FTSE 100 Index from the beginning of 1988 until December 1997, and they found that Monday returns are negative and generally the returns of the other four days of the week are significantly higher. Floros

(2008) rejects January effect for all the three indices which examined and he finds higher returns over other months rather January, but estimating coefficients are statistically insignificant, except significant negative returns in June for all indices. Mills *et al.* (2000) examine the month effect and found significant higher average returns on January and February. Choudhry (2001) reports significant negative returns in March and July for UK, while significant positive returns in February, August, September and December and significant negative returns in June and October were found for Germany. Aggarwal and Rivoli (1989) investigate the month –of-the-year effect and they find that January effects exist. The organization of the paper has as follows. In the section 2 we present the methodology which is followed. In section 3 we describe the nature of the data and we present the sources of them. In section 4 we present the results.

2. Methodology

2.1 The estimated model

In this section we present two simple models to examine the day-week effect and the second model is referred at the month of the year effect. The theoretical models have been derived by Panagiotidis and Alagidede (2006) which are

$$R_t = \phi_1 D_{1t} + \phi_2 D_{2t} + \phi_3 D_{3t} + \phi_4 D_{4t} + \phi_5 D_{5t} + n_i R_{t-1} + \varepsilon_\tau \qquad (1)$$

for the day of the week effect and

$$R_t = \sum_{i-1}^{12} \phi_i D_{it} + \varepsilon_\tau \qquad (2)$$

for the month of the year effect

, where R_t represent the returns of the General Index of Athens Stock Market R_{t-1} represent the general index with one lag. Also In model (1) the variables D_{1t} to D_{5t} are dummy variables and represent the days Monday to Friday and the dummy variables in model (2) express the months of the year. So for example in model (1) dummy variable D_{1t} obtains value 1 for Mondays and 0 otherwise and so on where finally dummy variable D_{5t} takes value 1 for returns on Fridays and 0 otherwise. Equations (1) and (2) are initially estimated with ordinary lest squares (OLS) method.

2.2 Symmetric and Asymmetric Generalized Autoregressive Conditional Heteroskedasticity-GARCH

Because the data we use in order to examine the day of the week effect are daily we expect that OLS method will present ARCH effects and autocorrelation. These problems can be eliminated by applying Generalized Autoregressive Conditional Heteroskedasticity-GARCH models. The first model we estimate is the symmetric GARCH(1,1) model proposed by Bollerslev (1987) and is defined as:

$$\varepsilon_t \mid \phi_{t-1} \sim N(0, \sigma^2_t) \tag{3}$$

$$\sigma_t^2 = \omega + a\varepsilon^2_{t-1} + \beta\sigma^2_{t-1} \tag{4}$$

, where ε_t is the disturbance term or residuals of equation (1) and follows the distribution in (3). GARCH (1,1) equation is presented in relation (4), where ω denotes the constant of variance equation GARCH and coefficients α and β express the ARCH and GARCH effects respectively. The problem with symmetric GARCH is that only squared residuals with lags enter the conditional variance equation, and then shocks have no effect on conditional volatility. With the symmetric GARCH we can't estimate the leverage effects. Leverage effects refer to the fact that "bad news" or negative shocks tend to have a larger impact on volatility than "good news" or positive shocks have. The first asymmetric GARCH we estimate is Exponential Generalized Autoregressive Conditional Heteroskedasticity-EGARCH (1,1) which was proposed by Nelson (1991) and is defined as:

$$\log(\sigma^2_t) = \omega + \log \beta(\sigma^2_{t-1}) + a\frac{u_{t-1}}{\sqrt{\sigma_{t-1}^2}} + \gamma\left[\frac{|u_{t-1}|}{\sqrt{\sigma_{t-1}^2}} - \sqrt{\frac{2}{\pi}}\right] \tag{5}$$

, where coefficient γ indicates the leverage effects.

The second asymmetric GARCH is Glosten-Jagannathan-Runkle Generalized Autoregressive Conditional Heteroskedasticity- GJR-GARCH (1,1) model proposed by Glosten *et al.* (1993). The variance equation is presented in (6).

$$\sigma_t^2 = \omega + a\varepsilon^2_{t-1} + \beta\sigma^2_{t-1} + \gamma\varepsilon^2_{t-1}I_{t-1} \tag{6}$$

3

I_{t-1} is a dummy variable , where $I_{t-1}=1$ if $u^2_{t-1}<0$ and $I_{t-1}=0$ otherwise. Also for a leverage effect we expect that $\gamma>0$ and we require $\alpha_1 + \gamma \geq 0$ and $\alpha_1 \geq 0$ for non-negativity condition. As in the case of EGARCH coefficient γ in GJR-GARCH equation indicates the leverage effects.

3. Data

The data for the day of the week effect are daily and for the month of the year are in monthly frequency. As we mentioned we examine the General Exchange Stock Market Index of Athens. For both calendar anomalies we examine the period $2^{nd\ t}$ January, 2002 to 30th October, 2007. The data are available at _www.enet.gr_.

4. Results

First of all we estimate the above models with the OLS method but we will test about heteroskedasticity and we will conclude that there are ARCH effects in the estimations for the day of the week effect. In an effort to eliminate this problem we estimate also with GARCH(1,1), GJR-GARCH (1,1) and EGARCH (1,1). The results are presented in appendix A . In table 1 the OLS estimations are reported. We conclude from the table 2 and the ARCH-LM test that the OLS is not the appropriate method to estimate this model. In tables 3, 4 and 5 the results of GARCH (1,1), GJR-GARCH (1,1) and EGARCH (1,1) respectively are presented.

For the GARCH(1,1) and the results of table 3 the sum of $\alpha_1 + \beta$ is almost 0.96 , which is smaller than unit and the GARCH β term is positive and statistically significant , as it's also in the GJR-GARCH (1,1) and EGARCH (1,1) estimations. The conclusion is that GARCH (1,1) is sufficient to capture the volatility clustering in the data and that shocks will be highly persistent in the conditional variance. Also in all models, including OLS, the AR(1) is positive and statistically significant. In GJR-GARCH (1,1) the parameter γ has the expected sign, which is positive and statistically significant and in EGARCH (1,1) parameter γ has also the correct and expected sign, which is negative and statistically significant indicating significant leverage effect in both models.

The general situation in all models is that there isn't day of the week effect, except Friday effect which coefficient is positive and statistically significant indicating 2,5-3,0% positive returns. In figures 1-3 presented the rolling regressions of OLS, GJR-GARCH and GARCH models separately are presented with 95% confidence intervals. We observe that coefficients are not stable and they present significant deviations and fluctuations around the mean. To be

4

specific while in the first half-period in rolling regressions negative returns are reported only on Monday in the second half-period Monday presents positive average returns, but the lowest average returns are reported on Tuesday, indicating that there is a change shift in the pattern of the day of the week effect. Generally there is only the Friday effect which this fact it is possible to explain that the Athens Stock market is not been characterized by market efficiency. Based on the period we examine as also the methodology we apply. On the other hand Friday effect depends on the ARCH effects, heteroskedasticity and autocorrelation, which after correcting this effect might be disappeared (Alagidede and Panagiotidis, 2006). But we observe that in GARCH and GJR-GARCH estimations only the coefficient representing Friday is a statistically significant, as also the coefficient of R_{t-1}, indicating that there significant average returns only on Friday and these are positive. In EGARCH estimations the results are quite different. Besides the two previous coefficients one additional coefficient is statistically significant, and it's the coefficient expressing Tuesday. Furthermore in $\alpha=0.10$ the highest and positive average returns are presented on Tuesday and not on Friday. But if we accept only in $\alpha=0.05$ and $\alpha=0.01$, then we reject the above statement, as Tuesday and Friday returns are statistically insignificant. However, we accept the estimations of GJR-GARCH, based on the Log-Likelihood statistic, which is the maximum among the various estimations, as also based on information criteria, Schwarz and Akaike, which are the minimum among all estimations.

For the month of the year effect the results are presented in table 6 with OLS method. Also in table 7 we apply the ARCH-LM test and in table 8 the correlogram of residuals squared are reported and we conclude that there aren't ARCH effects neither autocorrelation. We expected this phenomenon as the data we obtained to investigate about the month of the year effect are monthly. In the case we would had been taken daily data it would be very possible to found ARCH effects. So there isn't any need to estimate with GARCH models. In figure 4 the rolling estimates of the dummy variables with the OLS method with 95% confidence intervals are presented From figure 4 and the rolling OLS regressions for the month of the year effect we observe that in the first half-period the highest returns are not presented on January, but are reported on May, while in the second-half period January presents the highest returns. So we conclude that there is a change shift in the pattern of January or the month of the year effect. Moreover, in whole period March presents negative returns, while the average returns in November and December remain constant and always positive. Changes in the shift in the remained months are observed too.

The general situation is that there is the January effect, which is the only coefficient which is statistically significant in $\alpha=0.01$ and $\alpha=0.05$, as also November returns are statistically significant if we take α=0.10, but the average returns in January are higher than those of November. Also in appendix B we present the programming routine for the rolling regressions in EVIEWS software.

Conclusions

We examined the day of the week ad the month of the year effects for the Athens Stock market index and we found significant positive returns only on Friday. On the other hand we found significant highest positive returns in January and the returns in November are followed. The conclusion is that Athens exchange stock market might not be characterized by market efficiency, as calendar anomalies are presented. Another explanation of the presence of the calendar anomalies might be the methodology approach we follow. Additionally based on the rolling regressions we observe that in the half-period Monday presents negative returns, while positive returns are reported in the second half-period and the lowest returns are presented on Tuesday. Additionally, as we discussed in the main part of the study we concluded that there is a shift in the patter of the month of the year effect, where initially January presents positive average returns, but not the highest, while in the last months the highest and positive average returns are reported in January.

References

Agathee, U.S. (2008), "Day of the Week Effects: Evidence from the Stock Exchange of Mauritius (SEM)", *International Research Journal of Finance and Economics,* 17, 7-14

Aggarwal, R. and Rivoli, P. (1989), "Seasonal and Day-of-the-Week Effects in Four Emerging Stock Markets", *The Financial Review,* 24 (7), 541-550

Aggarwal, A. and Tandon, K. (1994), "Anomalies or illusions? Evidence from stock markets in eighteen countries", *Journal of International Money and Finance,* 13, 083-106

Alagidede, P. and Panagiotidis, T. (2006) "Calendar Anomalies in the Ghana Stock Exchange" Loughborough University, Department of economics Discussion paper series, WP 2006 – 13, U.K.

Bollerslev, T. (1986), "Generalized Autoregressive Conditional Heteroskedasticity" *Journal of Econometrics,* 31, 307-327

Choudhry, T. (2001), "Month of the year effect and January effect in Pre-WWI stock returns: Evidence from a non-linear GARCH model", *International Journal of Finance and Economics,* 6, 1-11

Draper, P. and Paudyal, K. (2002), "Explaining Monday returns", *The Journal of Financial Research,* 25 (4), 507–520

Floros, C. (2008), "The monthly and trading month effects in Greek stock market returns: 1996-2002", *Managerial Finance,* 34 (7), 453-464

Glosten, L. R., Jagannathan, R. and Runkle, D.E. (1993), "On the Relation between the Expected Value and the Volatility of the Nominal Excess Returns on Stocks", *Journal of Finance,* 48(5), 1779-1801

Mills, T.C. and Coutts, A.J. (1995), "Calendar effects in the London Stock Exchange FT-SE indices", *The European Journal of Finance,* 1, 79-93

Nelson, D.B. (1991), "Conditional Heteroskedasticity in Asset Returns: A new Approach", *Econometrica,* 59(2), 347-70

Table 1. OLS estimation of the day-week effect

Variable	Coefficient	Std. Error	t-Statistic	Prob.
SEAS1	-7.69E-06	0.000620	-0.012393	0.9901
SEAS2	0.000591	0.000618	0.955894	0.3393
SEAS3	-0.000125	0.000618	-0.202702	0.8394
SEAS4	0.000552	0.000618	0.892416	0.3723
SEAS5	0.001396	0.000618	2.257172	0.0241
LNGENERAL(-1)	0.067803	0.026277	2.580265	0.0100
R-squared	0.007109	Mean dependent var		0.000515
Adjusted R-squared	0.003657	S.D. dependent var		0.010529
S.E. of regression	0.010509	Akaike info criterion		-6.268936
Sum squared resid	0.158825	Schwarz criterion		-6.247017
Log likelihood	4532.172	Durbin-Watson stat		2.003204

*seas1 indicates Monday, seas2 indicates Tuesday and so on

Table 2. ARCH-LM test of the day-week effect

	p-value	*F-statistic*
ARCH with 1 lag	0.000799	11.29220
ARCH with 2 lags	0.000000	45.28827
ARCH with 3 lags	0.000000	35.82805
ARCH with 4 lags	0.000000	30.45886
ARCH with 5 lags	0.000000	25.87501

Table 3. GARCH (1,1) estimation of the day-week effect

	Coefficient	Std. Error	z-Statistic	Prob.
SEAS1	0.000459	0.000568	0.808213	0.4190
SEAS2	0.000919	0.000593	1.549693	0.1212
SEAS3	0.000469	0.000572	0.820653	0.4118
SEAS4	0.000712	0.000546	1.305425	0.1917
SEAS5	0.001326	0.000532	2.492312	0.0127
LNGENERAL(-1)	0.091518	0.030015	3.049105	0.0023
Variance Equation				
C	4.72E-06	1.33E-06	3.536594	0.0004
ARCH(1)	0.089217	0.013294	6.710857	0.0000
GARCH(1)	0.868127	0.020256	42.85877	0.0000
R-squared	0.005181	Mean dependent var		0.000515
Adjusted R-squared	-0.000365	S.D. dependent var		0.010529
S.E. of regression	0.010531	Akaike info criterion		-6.360930
Sum squared resid	0.159134	Schwarz criterion		-6.328051
Log likelihood	4601.591	Durbin-Watson stat		2.050028

Table 4. GJR-GARCH estimation of the day-week effect

	Coefficient	Std. Error	z-Statistic	Prob.
SEAS1	0.000237	0.000572	0.414638	0.6784
SEAS2	0.000782	0.000582	1.344193	0.1789
SEAS3	0.000320	0.000567	0.563439	0.5731
SEAS4	0.000594	0.000533	1.112606	0.2659
SEAS5	0.000918	0.000532	1.725172	0.0845
LNGENERAL(-1)	0.097846	0.030135	3.246914	0.0012
Variance Equation				
C	6.12E-06	1.58E-06	3.879726	0.0001
ARCH(1)	0.036757	0.013789	2.665692	0.0077
(RESID<0)*ARCH(1)	0.107777	0.022597	4.769614	0.0000
GARCH(1)	0.851404	0.024589	34.62503	0.0000
R-squared	0.005216	Mean dependent var		0.000515
Adjusted R-squared	-0.001027	S.D. dependent var		0.010529
S.E. of regression	0.010534	Akaike info criterion		-6.376115
Sum squared resid	0.159128	Schwarz criterion		-6.339583
Log likelihood	4613.555	Durbin-Watson stat		2.064402

* (RESID<0)*ARCH(1) indicates the leverage effects γ coefficient

Table 5. EGARCH estimation of the day-week effect

	Coefficient	Std. Error	z-Statistic	Prob.
SEAS1	0.000131	0.000568	0.230966	0.8173
SEAS2	0.000923	0.000553	1.668577	0.0952
SEAS3	0.000482	0.000555	0.868795	0.3850
SEAS4	0.000618	0.000529	1.168242	0.2427
SEAS5	0.000881	0.000535	1.648005	0.0994
LNGENERAL(-1)	0.093488	0.029371	3.182971	0.0015
Variance Equation				
C	-0.652129	0.136258	-4.785990	0.0000
|RES|/SQR[GARCH](1)	0.152625	0.026532	5.752498	0.0000
RES/SQR[GARCH](1)	-0.089157	0.016277	-5.477624	0.0000
EGARCH(1)	0.942314	0.013804	68.26553	0.0000
R-squared	0.005035	Mean dependent var		0.000515
Adjusted R-squared	-0.001210	S.D. dependent var		0.010529
S.E. of regression	0.010535	Akaike info criterion		-6.373379
Sum squared resid	0.159157	Schwarz criterion		-6.336848
Log likelihood	4611.580	Durbin-Watson stat		2.054892

* RES/SQR[GARCH](1) indicates the leverage effects γ coefficient

Figure 1. Rolling regression for OLS estimation of the day-week effect (initial sample 1000 and step size of 1; 450 observations for each coefficient)

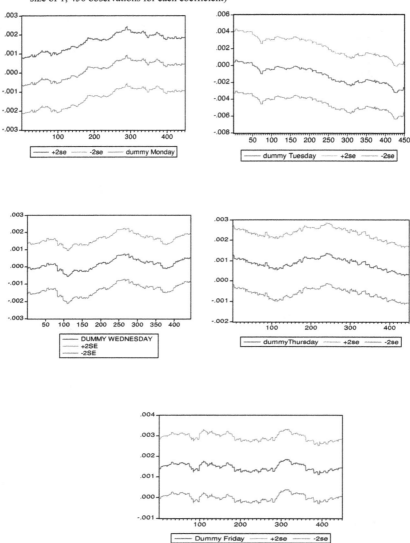

Figure 2. Rolling regression for GJR-GARCH (1,1) estimation of the day-week effect (initial sample 1000 and step size of 1; 445 observations for each coefficient)

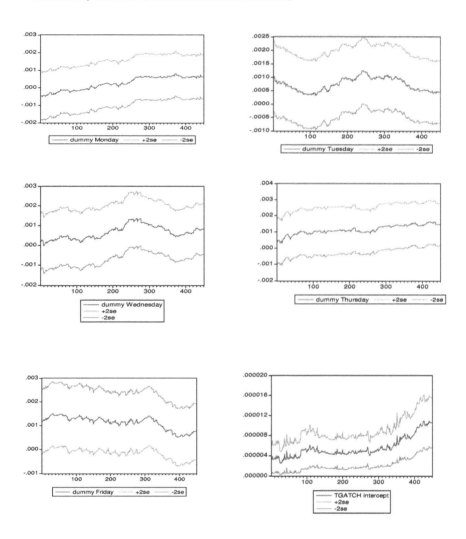

Figure 2. (Continue) Rolling regression for GJR-GARCH (1,1) estimation of the day-week effect (initial sample 1000 and step size of 1; 445 observations for each coefficient)

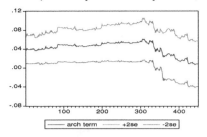

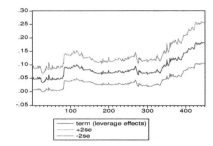

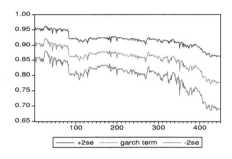

Figure 3. Rolling regression for GARCH (1,1)estimation of the day-week effect (initial sample 1000 and step size of 1; 445 observations for each coefficient)

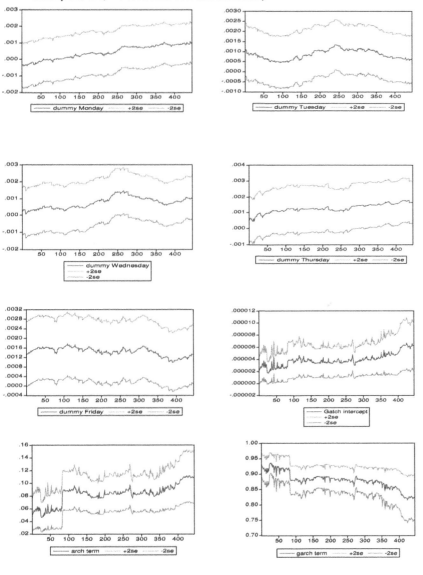

Table 6. OLS estimation of the month of the year effect

Variable	Coefficient	Std. Error	t-Statistic	Prob.
SEAS1	0.062032	0.022437	2.764736	0.0077
SEAS2	0.001196	0.020482	0.058375	0.9537
SEAS3	-0.030243	0.020482	-1.476578	0.1453
SEAS4	0.005075	0.020482	0.247778	0.8052
SEAS5	0.002530	0.020482	0.123529	0.9021
SEAS6	0.004861	0.020482	0.237329	0.8133
SEAS7	0.015448	0.020482	0.754218	0.4538
SEAS8	0.018879	0.020482	0.921724	0.3606
SEAS9	-0.012457	0.020482	-0.608220	0.5455
SEAS10	0.008556	0.020482	0.417714	0.6777
SEAS11	0.040534	0.022437	1.806602	0.0761
SEAS12	0.020536	0.022437	0.915274	0.3639
R-squared	0.188208	Mean dependent var		0.010124
Adjusted R-squared	0.031546	S.D. dependent var		0.050981
S.E. of regression	0.050170	Akaike info criterion		-2.990028
Sum squared resid	0.143471	Schwarz criterion		-2.601487
Log likelihood	115.1560	Durbin-Watson stat		1.499129

*seas1 indicates January, seas2 indicates February and so on up to seas12 which indicates December

Table 7. ARCH-LM test of the month of the year effect

	p-value	*F-statistic*
ARCH with 1 lag	0.974297	0.001046
ARCH with 2 lags	0.975820	0.024487

Table 8. Correlogram of residuals squared of OLS estimation for the month of the year effect

Autocorrelation	Partial Correlation		AC	PAC	Q-Stat	Prob
. | .	. | .	1	-0.004	-0.004	0.0011	0.973
. | .	. | .	2	0.027	0.027	0.0560	0.972
. |**	. |**	3	0.200	0.201	3.0381	0.386
. | .	. | .	4	0.061	0.065	3.3142	0.507
. |*.	. |*.	5	0.168	0.166	5.4750	0.361
. | .	. | .	6	0.034	0.000	5.5669	0.473
. | .	. | .	7	-0.016	-0.047	5.5862	0.589
. | .	. | .	8	0.049	-0.025	5.7780	0.672
. | .	. | .	9	-0.004	-0.034	5.7794	0.762
. | .	. | .	10	-0.029	-0.052	5.8493	0.828
. | .	. | .	11	0.020	0.011	5.8823	0.881
. | .	. | .	12	0.043	0.065	6.0407	0.914
.*| .	. | .	13	-0.070	-0.054	6.4649	0.928
. | .	. | .	14	0.018	0.022	6.4946	0.952
. | .	. | .	15	0.008	0.003	6.4999	0.970
. | .	. | .	16	-0.025	-0.012	6.5570	0.981
. | .	.*| .	17	-0.043	-0.067	6.7316	0.987
.*| .	.*| .	18	-0.073	-0.066	7.2488	0.988
. | .	. | .	19	-0.022	-0.026	7.2966	0.992
.*| .	. | .	20	-0.063	-0.054	7.6887	0.994
. | .	. | .	21	-0.030	0.015	7.7783	0.996
. | .	. | .	22	-0.007	0.036	7.7828	0.998
. | .	. | .	23	-0.042	0.006	7.9719	0.998
.*| .	. | .	24	-0.061	-0.046	8.3748	0.999
.*| .	.*| .	25	-0.072	-0.062	8.9577	0.999
. | .	.*| .	26	-0.052	-0.064	9.2675	0.999
.*| .	.*| .	27	-0.101	-0.107	10.446	0.998
.*| .	.*| .	28	-0.094	-0.076	11.509	0.997

Figure 4. Rolling regression for OLS estimation of the month of the year effect (initial sample 40 and step size of 1; 49 observations for each coefficient)

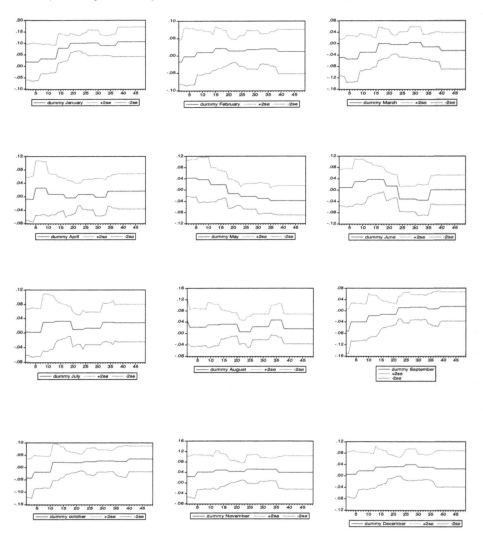

Appendix B

Programming routine in EVIEWS for the day of the week effect with rolling OLS

```
'Setting the OLS regression
equation eq1.ls lngeneral seas1 seas2 seas3 seas4 seas5 lngeneral(-1)
for !i = 1 to 450
smpl !i 1000+!i
equation res{!i}.ls lngeneral seas1 seas2 seas3 seas4 seas5 lngeneral(-1)


'Rolling coefficients for Monday returns
series seas1_dummy = res{!i}.@coefs(1)

'Rolling standard errors for Monday returns
series sig_seas1_hat= res{!i}.@stderrs(1)

'Rolling confidence intervals for Monday returns
series seas1_high= seas1_dummy+2*sig_seas1_hat
series seas1_low= seas1_dummy-2*sig_seas1_hat


'Rolling coefficients for Tuesday returns
series seas2_dummy = res{!i}.@coefs(2)

'Rolling standard errors for Tuesday returns
series sig_seas2_hat= res{!i}.@stderrs(2)

'Rolling confidence intervals for Tuesday returns
series seas2_high=seas2_dummy +2*sig_seas2_hat
series seas2_low=seas2_dummy -2*sig_seas2_hat

'Rolling coefficients for Wednesday returns
series seas3_dummy = res{!i}.@coefs(3)

'Rolling standard errors for Wednesday returns
series sig_seas3_hat= res{!i}.@stderrs(3)

'Rolling confidence intervals for Wednesday returns
series seas3_high=seas3_dummy +2*sig_seas3_hat
series seas3_low=seas3_dummy -2*sig_seas3_hat

'Rolling coefficients for Thursday returns
series seas4_dummy = res{!i}.@coefs(4)

'Rolling standard errors for Thursday returns
series sig_seas4_hat= res{!i}.@stderrs(4)


'Rolling confidence intervals for Thursday returns
series seas4_high=seas4_dummy +2*sig_seas4_hat
series seas4_low=seas4_dummy -2*sig_seas4_hat

'Rolling coefficients for Friday returns
series seas5_dummy = res{!i}.@coefs(5)

'Rolling standard errors for Friday returns
series sig_seas5_hat= res{!i}.@stderrs(5)

'Rolling confidence intervals for Friday returns
```

```
series seas5_high=seas5_dummy +2*sig_seas5_hat
series seas5_low=seas5_dummy -2*sig_seas5_hat
```

'Rolling coefficients for dependent variable with one lag
```
series lngeneral1 = res{!i}.@coefs(6)
```

'Rolling standard errors for dependent variable with one lag
```
series sig_hat_lngeneral1 = res{!i}.@stderrs(6)
```

'Rolling confidence intervals for dependent variable with one lag
```
series lngeneral1_high=lngeneral1 +2*sig_hat_lngeneral1
series lngeneral1_low=lngeneral1 -2*sig_hat_lngeneral1
```

```
next
```

```
smpl 1 450
graph graph1.line  seas1_dummy seas1_high seas1_low
graph graph2.line  seas2_dummy seas2_high seas2_low
graph graph3.line  seas3_dummy seas3_high seas3_low
graph graph4.line  seas4_dummy seas4_high seas4_low
graph graph5.line  seas5_dummy seas5_high seas5_low
graph graph6.line  lngeneral1 lngeneral1_high lngeneral1_low
```

Programming routine in EVIEWS for the day of the week effect with rolling GARCH(1,1)

'Setting the GARCH (1,1) regression
```
equation eq1.(arch,1,1) lngeneral seas1 seas2 seas3 seas4 seas5 lngeneral(-1)
for !i = 1 to 450
smpl !i 1000+!i
equation res{!i}.arch(1,1) lngeneral seas1 seas2 seas3 seas4 seas5 lngeneral(-1)
```

' The rolling coefficients for mean equation remain exactly the same as in the case of rolling OLS. The things that is changes is the variance equation, which in our case is GARCH (1,1)

'Rolling coefficients for constant of variance equation
```
series cons = res{!i}.@coefs(7)
```

'Rolling standard errors for constant of variance equation
```
series sig_hat_cons = res{!i}.@stderrs(7)
```

'Rolling confidence intervals for constant of variance equation
```
series cons_high=cons +2*sig_hat_cons
series cons_low=cons -2*sig_hat_cons
```

'Rolling coefficients for ARCH(1)
```
series arch1 = res{!i}.@coefs(8)
```

'Rolling standard errors for ARCH(1)
```
series sig_hat_arch1 = res{!i}.@stderrs(8)
```

'Rolling confidence intervals for ARCH(1)
```
series arch1_high=arch1 +2*sig_hat_arch1
series arch1_low=arch1 -2*sig_hat_arch1
```

'Rolling coefficients for GARCH(1)

```
series garch1 = res{li}.@coefs(9)

'Rolling standard errors for GARCH(1)
series sig_hat_garch1 = res{li}.@stderrs(9)

'Rolling confidence intervals for GARCH(1)
series garch1_high=garch1 +2*sig_hat_garch1
series garch1_low=garch1 -2*sig_hat_garch1

next

smpl 1 445

'Line graphs for mean equation coefficients
graph graph1.line  seas1_dummy seas1_high seas1_low
graph graph2.line  seas2_dummy seas2_high seas2_low
graph graph3.line  seas3_dummy seas3_high seas3_low
graph graph4.line  seas4_dummy seas4_high seas4_low
graph graph5.line  seas5_dummy seas5_high seas5_low
graph graph6.line  lngeneral1 lngeneral1_high lngeneral1_low

'Line graphs for variance equation coefficients
graph graph7.line  cons cons_high cons_low
graph graph8.line  arch1 arch1_high arch1_low
graph graph9.line  garch1 garch1_high garch1_low
```

Programming routine in EVIEWS for the day of the week effect with rolling EGARCH(1,1)

```
'Setting the EGARCH (1,1) regression
equation eq1.arch(e,egarch)     lngeneral seas1 seas2 seas3 seas4 seas5 lngeneral(-1)
for li = 1 to 450
smpl li 1000+li
equation res{li}.arch(e,egarch) lngeneral seas1 seas2 seas3 seas4 seas5 lngeneral(-1)
```

' The rolling coefficients for mean equation remain exactly the same as in the case of rolling OLS. The things that is changes is the variance equation, which in our case is EGARCH (1,1)

```
'Rolling coefficients for constant of variance equation
series cons = res{li}.@coefs(7)

'Rolling standard errors for constant of variance equation
series sig_hat_cons = res{li}.@stderrs(7)

'Rolling confidence intervals for constant of variance equation
series cons_high=cons +2*sig_hat_cons
series cons_low=cons -2*sig_hat_cons


'Rolling coefficients for ARCH(1)
series arch1 = res{li}.@coefs(8)

'Rolling standard errors for ARCH(1)
series sig_hat_arch1 = res{li}.@stderrs(8)

'Rolling confidence intervals for ARCH(1)
series arch1_high=arch1 +2*sig_hat_arch1
series arch1_low=arch1 -2*sig_hat_arch1
```

```
'Rolling coefficients for GARCH(1)
series garch1 = res{!i}.@coefs(9)

'Rolling standard errors for GARCH(1)
series sig_hat_garch1 = res{!i}.@stderrs(9)

'Rolling confidence intervals for GARCH(1)
series garch1_high=garch1 +2*sig_hat_garch1
series garch1_low=garch1 -2*sig_hat_garch1

'Rolling coefficients for EGARCH(1)
series egarch1 = res{!i}.@coefs(9)

'Rolling standard errors for EGARCH(1)
series sig_hat_egarch1 = res{!i}.@stderrs(9)

'Rolling confidence intervals for EGARCH(1)
series egarch1_high=egarch1 +2*sig_hat_egarch1
series egarch1_low=egarch1 -2*sig_hat_egarch1

next

smpl 1 445

'Line graphs for mean equation coefficients
graph graph1.line  seas1_dummy seas1_high seas1_low
graph graph2.line  seas2_dummy seas2_high seas2_low
graph graph3.line  seas3_dummy seas3_high seas3_low
graph graph4.line  seas4_dummy seas4_high seas4_low
graph graph5.line  seas5_dummy seas5_high seas5_low
graph graph6.line  lngeneral1 lngeneral1_high lngeneral1_low

'Line graphs for variance equation coefficients
graph graph7.line  cons cons_high cons_low
graph graph8.line  arch1 arch1_high arch1_low
graph graph9.line  garch1 garch1_high garch1_low
graph graph10.line egarch1 egarch1_high egarch1_low
```

Programming routine in EVIEWS for the day of the week effect with rolling GJR-GARCH(1,1)

```
'Setting the GJR-GARCH (1,1) regression
equation eq1.arch(t,tarch)        lngeneral seas1 seas2 seas3 seas4 seas5 lngeneral(-1)
for !i = 1 to 450
smpl !i 1000+!i
equation res{!i}.arch(t,tarch) lngeneral seas1 seas2 seas3 seas4 seas5 lngeneral(-1)

' The rolling coefficients for mean equation remain exactly the same as in the case of rolling OLS. The
things that is changes is the variance equation, which in our case is GJR-GARCH (1,1)

'Rolling coefficients for constant of variance equation
series cons = res{!i}.@coefs(7)

'Rolling standard errors for constant of variance equation
series sig_hat_cons = res{!i}.@stderrs(7)

'Rolling confidence intervals for constant of variance equation
series cons_high=cons +2*sig_hat_cons
```

```
series cons_low=cons -2*sig_hat_cons


'Rolling coefficients for ARCH(1)
series arch1 = res{!i}.@coefs(8)

'Rolling standard errors for ARCH(1)
series sig_hat_arch1 = res{!i}.@stderrs(8)

'Rolling confidence intervals for ARCH(1)
series arch1_high=arch1 +2*sig_hat_arch1
series arch1_low=arch1 -2*sig_hat_arch1


'Rolling coefficients for GARCH(1)
series garch1 = res{!i}.@coefs(9)

'Rolling standard errors for GARCH(1)
series sig_hat_garch1 = res{!i}.@stderrs(9)

'Rolling confidence intervals for GARCH(1)
series garch1_high=garch1 +2*sig_hat_garch1
series garch1_low=garch1 -2*sig_hat_garch1

'Rolling coefficients for TGARCH(1)
series tgarch1 = res{!i}.@coefs(9)

'Rolling standard errors for TGARCH (1)
series sig_hat_ tgarch1 = res{!i}.@stderrs(9)

'Rolling confidence intervals for TGARCH (1)
series tgarch1 _high= tgarch1 +2*sig_hat_ tgarch1
series tgarch1 _low= tgarch1 -2*sig_hat_ tgarch1

next


smpl 1 445

'Line graphs for mean equation coefficients
graph graph1.line  seas1_dummy seas1_high seas1_low
graph graph2.line  seas2_dummy seas2_high seas2_low
graph graph3.line  seas3_dummy seas3_high seas3_low
graph graph4.line  seas4_dummy seas4_high seas4_low
graph graph5.line  seas5_dummy seas5_high seas5_low
graph graph6.line  lngeneral1 lngeneral1_high lngeneral1_low

'Line graphs for variance equation coefficients
graph graph7.line  cons cons_high cons_low
graph graph8.line  arch1 arch1_high arch1_low
graph graph9.line  garch1 garch1_high garch1_low
graph graph10.line tgarch1 tgarch1_high tgarch1_low
```

Programming routine in EVIEWS for the month of the year effect with rolling OLS

```
equation eq1.ls lngeneral seas1 seas2 seas3 seas4 seas5 seas6 seas7 seas8 seas9 seas10 seas11
seas12
for !i = 1 to 40
smpl !i 30+!i
equation res{!i}.ls lngeneral seas1 seas2 seas3 seas4 seas5 seas6 seas7 seas8 seas9 seas10
seas11 seas12
```

'Rolling coefficients for January returns
series m1= res{!i}.@coefs(1)

'Rolling standard errors for January returns
series sig1hat= res{!i}.@stderrs(1)

'Rolling confidence intervals for January returns
series m1_high= m1+2* sig1hat
series m1_low= m1-2* sig1hat

'Rolling coefficients for February returns
series m2= res{!i}.@coefs(2)

'Rolling standard errors for February returns
series sig2hat= res{!i}.@stderrs(2)

'Rolling confidence intervals for February returns
series m2_high= m2+2* sig2hat
series m2_low= m2-2* sig2hat

'Rolling coefficients for March returns
series m3= res{!i}.@coefs(3)

'Rolling standard errors for March returns
series sig3hat= res{!i}.@stderrs(3)

'Rolling confidence intervals for March returns
series m3_high= m3+2* sig3hat
series m3_low= m3-2* sig3hat

'Rolling coefficients for April returns
series m4= res{!i}.@coefs(4)

'Rolling standard errors for April returns
series sig4hat= res{!i}.@stderrs(4)

'Rolling confidence intervals for April returns
series m4_high= m4+2* sig4hat
series m4_low= m4-2* sig4hat

'Rolling coefficients for May returns
series m5= res{!i}.@coefs(5)

'Rolling standard errors for May returns
series sig5hat= res{!i}.@stderrs(5)

'Rolling confidence intervals for May returns
series m5_high= m5+2* sig5hat
series m5_low= m5-2* sig5hat

'Rolling coefficients for June returns
series m6= res{!i}.@coefs(6)

'Rolling standard errors for June returns
series sig6hat= res{!i}.@stderrs(6)

'Rolling confidence intervals for June returns
series m6_high= m6+2* sig6hat
series m6_low= m6-2* sig6hat

```
'Rolling coefficients for July returns
series m7= res{!i}.@coefs(7)

'Rolling standard errors for July returns
series sig7hat= res{!i}.@stderrs(7)

'Rolling confidence intervals for July returns
series m7_high=m7+2*sig7hat
series m7_low=m7-2*sig7hat

'Rolling coefficients for August returns
series m8= res{!i}.@coefs(8)

'Rolling standard errors for August returns
series sig8hat= res{!i}.@stderrs(8)

'Rolling confidence intervals for August returns
series m8_high=m8+2*sig8hat
series m8_low=m8-2*sig8hat

'Rolling coefficients for September returns
series m9= res{!i}.@coefs(9)

'Rolling standard errors for September returns
series sig9hat= res{!i}.@stderrs(9)

'Rolling confidence intervals for September returns
series m9_high=m9+2*sig9hat
series m9_low=m9-2*sig9hat


'Rolling coefficients for October returns
series m10= res{!i}.@coefs(10)

'Rolling standard errors for October returns
series sig10hat= res{!i}.@stderrs(10)


'Rolling confidence intervals for October returns
series m10_high=m10+2*sig10hat
series m10_low=m10-2*sig10hat

'Rolling coefficients for November returns
series m11= res{!i}.@coefs(11)

'Rolling standard errors for November returns
series sig11hat= res{!i}.@stderrs(11)

'Rolling confidence intervals for November returns
series m11_high=m11+2*sig11hat
series m11_low=m11-2*sig11hat

'Rolling coefficients for December returns
series m12= res{!i}.@coefs(12)

'Rolling standard errors for December returns
series sig12hat= res{!i}.@stderrs(12)

'Rolling confidence intervals for December returns
series m12_high=m12+2*sig12hat
```

```
series m12_low=m12-2*sig12hat

smpl 1 40
graph graph1.line  m1 m1_high m1_low
graph graph2.line  m2 m2_high m2_low
graph graph3.line  m3 m3_high m3_low
graph graph4.line  m4 m4_high m4_low
graph graph5.line  m5 m5_high m5_low
graph graph6.line  m6 m6_high m6_low
graph graph7.line  m7 m7_high m7_low
graph graph8.line  m8 m8 _high m8_low
graph graph9.line  m9 m9 _high m9_low
graph graph10.line  m10 m10_high m10_low
graph graph11.line  m11 m11_high m11_low
graph graph12.line  m112 m12_high m12_low
```

In a similar way GARCH models are estimated as in the case of the day of the week effect. We present an example only for GARCH (1,1)

Programming routine in EVIEWS for the month of the year effect with rolling GARCH(1,1)

```
'Rolling coefficients for constant of variance equation
series cons =  res{!i}.@coefs(13)

'Rolling standard errors for constant of variance equation
series sig_hat_cons  =  res{!i}.@stderrs(13)

'Rolling confidence intervals for constant of variance equation
series cons_high=cons +2*sig_hat_cons
series cons_low=cons -2*sig_hat_cons


'Rolling coefficients for ARCH(1)
series arch1 =  res{!i}.@coefs(14)

'Rolling standard errors for ARCH(1)
series sig_hat_arch1  =  res{!i}.@stderrs(14)

'Rolling confidence intervals for ARCH(1)
series arch1_high=arch1 +2*sig_hat_arch1
series arch1_low=arch1 -2*sig_hat_arch1


'Rolling coefficients for GARCH(1)
series garch1 =  res{!i}.@coefs(15)

'Rolling standard errors for GARCH(1)
series sig_hat_garch1  =  res{!i}.@stderrs(15)

'Rolling confidence intervals for GARCH(1)
series garch1_high=garch1 +2*sig_hat_garch1
series garch1_low=garch1 -2*sig_hat_garch1

next
```

```
smpl 1 40

'Line graphs for mean equation coefficients
graph graph1.line  m1 m1_high m1_low
graph graph2.line  m2 m2_high m2_low
graph graph3.line  m3 m3_high m3_low
graph graph4.line  m4 m4_high m4_low
graph graph5.line  m5 m5_high m5_low
graph graph6.line  m6 m6_high m6_low
graph graph7.line  m7 m7_high m7_low
graph graph8.line  m8 m8 _high m8_low
graph graph9.line  m9 m9 _high m9_low
graph graph10.line  m10 m10_high m10_low
graph graph11.line  m11 m11_high m11_low
graph graph12.line  m112 m12_high m12_low

'Line graphs for variance equation coefficients
graph graph13.line  cons cons_high cons_low
graph graph14.line  arch1 arch1_high arch1_low
graph graph15.line  garch1 garch1_high garch1_low
```

Programming Routines for OLS and GARCH rolling regressions in MATLAB

```
clear all;
load file.mat

window=445      % the window sample for rolling regressions

em=4     % Estimated method 1 for OLS, 2 for GARCH, 3 for EGARCH,
         % 4 for GJR-GARCH
Dist='Gaussian' % Gaussian or T distribution
P=1 %Order for ARCH component
Q=1 %Order for GARCH component


% size of y
[ni,no]=size(y);

% y a vector of dependent  variable, while x is the matrix of dummy variables
% Take on lag of dependent  variable
y_lag=lagmatrix(y,1)

% We exclude NaN values by obtaining before the lag
i1 = find(isnan(y_lag));
i2 = find(isnan(diff([y_lag ; zeros(1,size(y_lag,2))]) .* y_lag));
if (length(i1) ~= length(i2)) || any(i1 - i2)
  error('Series cannot contain NaN).')
end

if any(sum(isnan(y_lag)) == size(y_lag,1))
  error('A realization of "x" is completely missing (all NaN"s).')
end

first_Row = max(sum(isnan(y_lag))) + 1;
y_lag      = y_lag(first_Row:end , :);
y=y(first_Row:end , :);
x=x(first_Row:end , :);

% The new matrix of indepedent variables, including dummy and the lag of the
```

```
% depedent variable.
x=[x,y_lag]

% loop for rolling regression
if em==1    % OLS
for i=window:ni-1
    for q = 1:ni-window+1;


y1=y(q:i,:)
x1=x(q:i,:)


bols(:,i) = inv(x1'*x1)*x1'*y1   % estimated rolling coefficients
s2(:,i) = (y1-x1*bols(:,i))'*(y1-x1*bols(:,i))/(ni-no)

se(:,i)=sqrt(diag(s2(:,i)*inv(x1'*x1))); % get coefficient standard errors


tstudent(:,i)=bols(:,i)./se(:,i);   % Get t-student statistics

% rolling confidense intervals
upper_limit(:,i)=bols(:,i)+1.96*se(:,i)
lower_limit(:,i)=bols(:,i)-1.96*se(:,i)
end
end

% Line plot for Monday returns
subplot(3,2,1),  plot(upper_limit(1,window:ni-1),'r'); hold on;...
    plot(lower_limit(1,window:ni-1),'b'); plot(bols(1,window:ni-1),'g')
title('Monday')
% Line plot for Tuesday returns
subplot(3,2,2),plot(upper_limit(2,window:ni-1),'r'); hold on;...
    plot(lower_limit(2,window:ni-1),'b'); plot(bols(2,window:ni-1),'g')
title('Tuesday')
% Line plot for Wednesday returns
subplot(3,2,3),  plot(upper_limit(3,window:ni-1),'r'); hold on;...
    plot(lower_limit(3,window:ni-1),'b'); plot(bols(3,window:ni-1),'g')
title('Wednesday')
% Line plot for Thursday returns
subplot(3,2,4),plot(upper_limit(4,window:ni-1),'r'); hold on;...
    plot(lower_limit(4,window:ni-1),'b'); plot(bols(4,window:ni-1),'g')
title('Thursday')
% Line plot for Friday returns
subplot(3,2,5),  plot(upper_limit(5,window:ni-1),'r'); hold on;...
    plot(lower_limit(5,window:ni-1),'b'); plot(bols(5,window:ni-1),'g')
title('Friday')
% Line plot for dependent variable with lag returns
subplot(3,2,6),plot(upper_limit(6,window:ni-1),'r'); hold on;...
    plot(lower_limit(6,window:ni-1),'b'); plot(bols(6,window:ni-1),'g')
title('lag(1)')


elseif em==2    % GARCH
spec = garchset('VarianceModel', GARCH,'Distribution',Dist,'P', P,'Q',...
Q,'C',NaN,'Display','off')

for i=window:ni-1
    for q = 1:ni-window+1;
y1=y(q:i,:)
x1=x(q:i,:)
```

```
% GARCH estimation
[Coeff,Errors] =garchfit(spec,y1,x1)

%------------Mean Equation------------%
% Estimated rolling coefficients
bols(:,i)=Coeff.Regress'

% Estimated standard errors
se(:,i)=Errors.Regress'

% rolling confidense intervals
upper_limit(:,i)=bols(:,i)+1.96*se(:,i)
lower_limit(:,i)=bols(:,i)-1.96*se(:,i)



%------------ Variance Equation-----------%
% Rolling constant of variance equation
K1(:,i)=Coeff.K
% Rolling standard errors for constant of variance equation
K_se1(:,i)=Errors.K
% rolling confidenses intervals for constant of variance equation
upper_limit_K1(:,i)=K1(:,i)+1.96*K_se1(:,i)
lower_limit_K1(:,i)=K1(:,i)-1.96*K_se1(:,i)

% Rolling ARCH coefficients of variance equation
ARCH1(:,i)=Coeff.ARCH
% Rolling standard errors for ARCH coefficients  of variance equation
ARCH_se(:,i)=Errors.ARCH
% rolling confidenses intervals for ARCH coefficients of variance equation
upper_limit_ARCH1(:,i)=ARCH1(:,i)+1.96*ARCH_se(:,i)
lower_limit_ARCH1(:,i)=ARCH1(:,i)-1.96*ARCH_se(:,i)


% Rolling GARCH coefficients of variance equation
GARCH1(:,i)=Coeff.GARCH
% Rolling standard errors for GARCH coefficients of variance equation
GARCH_se(:,i)=Errors.GARCH
% rolling confidenses intervals for GARCH coefficients of variance equation
upper_limit_GARCH1(:,i)=GARCH1(:,i)+1.96*GARCH_se(:,i)
lower_limit_GARCH1(:,i)=GARCH1(:,i)-1.96*GARCH_se(:,i)
 end
end
% Line plot for Monday returns
subplot(3,4,1),  plot(upper_limit(1,window:ni-1),'r'); hold on;...
    plot(lower_limit(1,window:ni-1),'b'); plot(bols(1,window:ni-1),'g')
title('Monday')
% Line plot for Tuesday returns
subplot(3,4,2),plot(upper_limit(2,window:ni-1),'r'); hold on;...
    plot(lower_limit(2,window:ni-1),'b'); plot(bols(2,window:ni-1),'g')
title('Tuesday')
% Line plot for Wednesday returns
subplot(3,4,3), plot(upper_limit(3,window:ni-1),'r'); hold on;...
    plot(lower_limit(3,window:ni-1),'b'); plot(bols(3,window:ni-1),'g')
title('Wednesday')
% Line plot for Thursday returns
subplot(3,4,4),plot(upper_limit(4,window:ni-1),'r'); hold on;...
    plot(lower_limit(4,window:ni-1),'b'); plot(bols(4,window:ni-1),'g')
title('Thursday')
% Line plot for Friday returns
subplot(3,4,5), plot(upper_limit(5,window:ni-1),'r'); hold on;...
    plot(lower_limit(5,window:ni-1),'b'); plot(bols(5,window:ni-1),'g')
```

```matlab
title('Friday')
% Line plot for dependent variable with lag returns
subplot(3,4,6),plot(upper_limit(6,window:ni-1),'r'); hold on;...
   plot(lower_limit(6,window:ni-1),'b'); plot(bols(6,window:ni-1),'g')
title('lag(1)')

% Line plot for constant of variance equation
subplot(3,4,7),plot(upper_limit_K1(:,window:ni-1),'r'); hold on;...
   plot(lower_limit_K1(:,window:ni-1),'b'); plot(K1(:,window:ni-1),'g')
title('constant')

% Line plot for ARCH coefficients of variance equation
subplot(3,4,8),plot(upper_limit_ARCH1(:,window:ni-1),'r'); hold on;...
   plot(lower_limit_ARCH1(:,window:ni-1),'b'); plot(ARCH1(:,window:ni-1),'g')
title('ARCH')

% Line plot for GARCH coefficients of variance equation
subplot(3,4,9),plot(upper_limit_GARCH1(:,window:ni-1),'r'); hold on;...
   plot(lower_limit_GARCH1(:,window:ni-1),'b'); plot(GARCH1(:,window:ni-1),'g')
title('GARCH')


elseif em==3    % EGARCH

spec = garchset('VarianceModel','EGARCH','Distribution',Dist,'P', P,...
'Q', Q,'C',NaN,'Display','off')

for i=window:ni-1
    for q = 1:ni-window+1;
y1=y(q:i,:)
x1=x(q:i,:)

% GARCH estimation
[Coeff,Errors] =garchfit(spec,y1,x1)

%------------Mean Equation-------------%
% Estimated rolling coefficients
bols(:,i)=Coeff.Regress'

% Estimated standard errors
se(:,i)=Errors.Regress'

% rolling confidense intervals
upper_limit(:,i)=bols(:,i)+1.96*se(:,i)
lower_limit(:,i)=bols(:,i)-1.96*se(:,i)

%------------ Variance Equation-----------%
% Rolling constant of variance equation
K1(:,i)=Coeff.K
% Rolling standard errors for constant of variance equation
K_se1(:,i)=Errors.K
% rolling confidenses intervals for constant of variance equation
upper_limit_K1(:,i)=K1(:,i)+1.96*K_se1(:,i)
lower_limit_K1(:,i)=K1(:,i)-1.96*K_se1(:,i)

% Rolling ARCH coefficients of variance equation
ARCH1(:,i)=Coeff.ARCH
% Rolling standard errors for ARCH coefficients  of variance equation
ARCH_se(:,i)=Errors.ARCH
% rolling confidenses intervals for ARCH coefficients of variance equation
upper_limit_ARCH1(:,i)=ARCH1(:,i)+1.96*ARCH_se(:,i)
```

```
lower_limit_ARCH1(:,i)=ARCH1(:,i)-1.96*ARCH_se(:,i)


% Rolling GARCH coefficients of variance equation
GARCH1(:,i)=Coeff.GARCH
% Rolling standard errors for GARCH coefficients of variance equation
GARCH_se(:,i)=Errors.GARCH
% rolling confidenses intervals for GARCH coefficients of variance equation
upper_limit_GARCH1(:,i)=GARCH1(:,i)+1.96*GARCH_se(:,i)
lower_limit_GARCH1(:,i)=GARCH1(:,i)-1.96*GARCH_se(:,i)

% Rolling coefficients of Leverage effects of variance equation
Leverage1(:,i)=Coeff.Leverage

% Rolling standard errors for Leverage effects coefficients of variance equation
Leverage_se1(:,i)=Errors.Leverage

% rolling confidenses intervals for Leverage effects coefficients of
% variance equation
upper_limit_Leverage1(:,i)=Leverage1(:,i)+1.96*Leverage_se1(:,i)
lower_limit_Leverage1(:,i)=Leverage1(:,i)-1.96*Leverage_se1(:,i)

    end
end
% Line plot for Monday returns
subplot(3,4,1),  plot(upper_limit(1,window:ni-1),'r'); hold on;...
    plot(lower_limit(1,window:ni-1),'b'); plot(bols(1,window:ni-1),'g')
title('Monday')
% Line plot for Tuesday returns
subplot(3,4,2),plot(upper_limit(2,window:ni-1),'r'); hold on;...
    plot(lower_limit(2,window:ni-1),'b'); plot(bols(2,window:ni-1),'g')
title('Tuesday')
% Line plot for Wednesday returns
subplot(3,4,3), plot(upper_limit(3,window:ni-1),'r'); hold on;...
    plot(lower_limit(3,window:ni-1),'b'); plot(bols(3,window:ni-1),'g')
title('Wednesday')
% Line plot for Thursday returns
subplot(3,4,4),plot(upper_limit(4,window:ni-1),'r'); hold on;...
    plot(lower_limit(4,window:ni-1),'b'); plot(bols(4,window:ni-1),'g')
title('Thursday')
% Line plot for Friday returns
subplot(3,4,5), plot(upper_limit(5,window:ni-1),'r'); hold on;...
    plot(lower_limit(5,window:ni-1),'b'); plot(bols(5,window:ni-1),'g')
title('Friday')
% Line plot for dependent variable with lag returns
subplot(3,4,6),plot(upper_limit(6,window:ni-1),'r'); hold on;...
    plot(lower_limit(6,window:ni-1),'b'); plot(bols(6,window:ni-1),'g')
title('lag(1)')

% Line plot for constant of variance equation
subplot(3,4,7),plot(upper_limit_K1(:,window:ni-1),'r'); hold on;...
    plot(lower_limit_K1(:,window:ni-1),'b'); plot(K1(:,window:ni-1),'g')
title('constant')

% Line plot for ARCH coefficients of variance equation
subplot(3,4,8),plot(upper_limit_ARCH1(:,window:ni-1),'r'); hold on;...
    plot(lower_limit_ARCH1(:,window:ni-1),'b'); plot(ARCH1(:,window:ni-1),'g')
title('ARCH')

% Line plot for GARCH coefficients of variance equation
subplot(3,4,9),plot(upper_limit_GARCH1(:,window:ni-1),'r'); hold on;...
    plot(lower_limit_GARCH1(:,window:ni-1),'b'); plot(GARCH1(:,window:ni-1),'g')
```

```matlab
title('GARCH')

% Line plot for Leverage effects coefficients of variance equation
subplot(3,4,10),plot(upper_limit_Leverage1(:,window:ni-1),'r'); hold on;...
    plot(lower_limit_Leverage1(:,window:ni-1),'b'); plot(Leverage1(:,window:ni-1),'g')
title('Leverage')

elseif em==4  % GJR-GARCH

   spec = garchset('VarianceModel','GJR','Distribution',Dist,'P', P,...
'Q', Q,'C',NaN,'Display','off')
 for i=window:ni-1
    for q = 1:ni-window+1;
y1=y(q:i,:)
x1=x(q:i,:)

% GARCH estimation
[Coeff,Errors] =garchfit(spec,y1,x1)

%------------Mean Equation-------------%
% Estimated rolling coefficients
bols(:,i)=Coeff.Regress'

% Estimated standard errors
se(:,i)=Errors.Regress'

% rolling confidense intervals
upper_limit(:,i)=bols(:,i)+1.96*se(:,i)
lower_limit(:,i)=bols(:,i)-1.96*se(:,i)

   %------------ Variance Equation-----------%
% Rolling constant of variance equation
K1(:,i)=Coeff.K
% Rolling standard errors for constant of variance equation
K_se1(:,i)=Errors.K
% rolling confidenses intervals for constant of variance equation
upper_limit_K1(:,i)=K1(:,i)+1.96*K_se1(:,i)
lower_limit_K1(:,i)=K1(:,i)-1.96*K_se1(:,i)

% Rolling ARCH coefficients of variance equation
ARCH1(:,i)=Coeff.ARCH
% Rolling standard errors for ARCH coefficients  of variance equation
ARCH_se(:,i)=Errors.ARCH
% rolling confidenses intervals for ARCH coefficients of variance equation
upper_limit_ARCH1(:,i)=ARCH1(:,i)+1.96*ARCH_se(:,i)
lower_limit_ARCH1(:,i)=ARCH1(:,i)-1.96*ARCH_se(:,i)


% Rolling GARCH coefficients of variance equation
GARCH1(:,i)=Coeff.GARCH
% Rolling standard errors for GARCH coefficients of variance equation
GARCH_se(:,i)=Errors.GARCH
% rolling confidenses intervals for GARCH coefficients of variance equation
upper_limit_GARCH1(:,i)=GARCH1(:,i)+1.96*GARCH_se(:,i)
lower_limit_GARCH1(:,i)=GARCH1(:,i)-1.96*GARCH_se(:,i)

% Rolling coefficients of Leverage effects of variance equation
Leverage1(:,i)=Coeff.Leverage

% Rolling standard errors for Leverage effects coefficients of variance equation
Leverage_se1(:,i)=Errors.Leverage
```

```
% rolling confidenses intervals for Leverage effects coefficients of
% variance equation
upper_limit_Leverage1(:,i)=Leverage1(:,i)+1.96*Leverage_se1(:,i)
lower_limit_Leverage1(:,i)=Leverage1(:,i)-1.96*Leverage_se1(:,i)

    end
  end
 % Line plot for Monday returns
subplot(3,4,1), plot(upper_limit(1,window:ni-1),'r'); hold on;...
    plot(lower_limit(1,window:ni-1),'b'); plot(bols(1,window:ni-1),'g')
title('Monday')
% Line plot for Tuesday returns
subplot(3,4,2),plot(upper_limit(2,window:ni-1),'r'); hold on;...
    plot(lower_limit(2,window:ni-1),'b'); plot(bols(2,window:ni-1),'g')
title('Tuesday')
% Line plot for Wednesday returns
subplot(3,4,3), plot(upper_limit(3,window:ni-1),'r'); hold on;...
    plot(lower_limit(3,window:ni-1),'b'); plot(bols(3,window:ni-1),'g')
title('Wednesday')
% Line plot for Thursday returns
subplot(3,4,4),plot(upper_limit(4,window:ni-1),'r'); hold on;...
    plot(lower_limit(4,window:ni-1),'b'); plot(bols(4,window:ni-1),'g')
title('Thursday')
% Line plot for Friday returns
subplot(3,4,5), plot(upper_limit(5,window:ni-1),'r'); hold on;...
    plot(lower_limit(5,window:ni-1),'b'); plot(bols(5,window:ni-1),'g')
title('Friday')
% Line plot for dependent variable with lag returns
subplot(3,4,6),plot(upper_limit(6,window:ni-1),'r'); hold on;...
    plot(lower_limit(6,window:ni-1),'b'); plot(bols(6,window:ni-1),'g')
title('lag(1)')

% Line plot for constant of variance equation
subplot(3,4,7),plot(upper_limit_K1(:,window:ni-1),'r'); hold on;...
    plot(lower_limit_K1(:,window:ni-1),'b'); plot(K1(:,window:ni-1),'g')
title('constant')

% Line plot for ARCH coefficients of variance equation
subplot(3,4,8),plot(upper_limit_ARCH1(:,window:ni-1),'r'); hold on;...
    plot(lower_limit_ARCH1(:,window:ni-1),'b'); plot(ARCH1(:,window:ni-1),'g')
title('ARCH')

% Line plot for GARCH coefficients of variance equation
subplot(3,4,9),plot(upper_limit_GARCH1(:,window:ni-1),'r'); hold on;...
    plot(lower_limit_GARCH1(:,window:ni-1),'b'); plot(GARCH1(:,window:ni-1),'g')
title('GARCH')

% Line plot for Leverage effects coefficients of variance equation
subplot(3,4,10),plot(upper_limit_Leverage1(:,window:ni-1),'r'); hold on;...
    plot(lower_limit_Leverage1(:,window:ni-1),'b'); plot(Leverage1(:,window:ni-1),'g')
title('Leverage')

end
```

YOUR KNOWLEDGE HAS VALUE

www.ingramcontent.com/pod-product-compliance
Lightning Source LLC
La Vergne TN
LVHW042307060326
832902LV00009B/1313